Old Age Signs And Love

How to prepare yourself and embrace the end of lifetime mystery.

Donald J. Houston

Old Age Signs
And Love

How to prepare yourself and embrace the end of lifetime mystery.

Donald J. Houston

Table of content

Chapter 1

Aging gracefully according to your zodiac sign

Is it inscribed in the stars how you age? We don't know, but it's entertaining to speculate. Here are our wildly speculative predictions for how the zodiac signs will mature.

Zodiac Signs and Aging

Aquarius

You like pondering the future and are an early adopter of new concepts. When others get stale, that approach to life will keep you fresh. You enjoy intellectual stimulation and problem solving, so use your sharp mind to figure out what your body need in terms of diet and exercise – it will pay you handsomely as the years pass. Be aware that Aquarius women have a tendency to bottle up their emotions, and focus on expressing them for improved mental health.

Pisces

Little fishes move with the flow and enjoy interacting with others. This might seem like late nights after late nights spent overindulging at parties in your early years. That takes a toll on the body, so if you want to age gracefully, you'll have to step up your game later in life. Redirect that social energy into activities that are both entertaining and healthful, such as dancing lessons and charity work. The good news is that people who have a large number of friends live longer and are happier.

Taurus

You are a hedonist who loves all the good things: rich food, fine clothes, counting the stars, and seeing every sunrise. Moderation has never been part of your vocabulary. Your philosophy: Who wants to live to be

100 if that means giving up caffeine, alcohol, and sugar? However, you may find that as you grow older, you enjoy a bit of a slower pace. Still, you will never miss a chance to smell the roses.

Aries

You have the stamina to live a long and healthy life if you have boundless energy. Your tenacity pays off because you're willing to figure out what it takes to be your best at any age and then put in the effort to achieve it. Don't be too hard on yourself when your young attractiveness transforms into a more mature appearance. Your inner radiance will always be visible. Exploration and adventure are important to Aries, so keep them in mind.

Gemini

Your sign embodies duality, and you're living proof that youth is a state of mind rather than a number. Your pendulum personality may not swing as wide as it once did as you become older, but you'll never lose that lovely Gemini vitality. You'll always be the first to sign up for something new because of your busy intellect and love of trends. For the rest of your life, that trait will keep you one step ahead of the competition.

Cancer

Cancers are creatures of habit and tradition. Yours should be centered on health and wellness. You find it simple to exercise and eat healthily on a daily basis. Cancer patients require a great deal of compassion and care from both themselves and others. Treat yourself with respect and allow yourself to be loved for the rest of your life. Friendships and family ties should be nurtured. Those techniques, when combined, almost guarantee that you will age gracefully.

Leo

Laughter is the best medicine, and you've had enough of it in your life, Leo. Your sense of humour will help you get through the difficult moments that come with becoming older. Because you're a fire sign, you've definitely spent much too much time in the sun. Hopefully, you took everyone's advice and wore sunscreen. However, if you don't have wrinkles, you can probably pass them off as laugh lines. We admire you because you don't take ageism lightly.

Virgo

Structure is important to Virgos in their life, including eating and exercise, since it allows them to focus on the details — and by details, we mean concern. Worrying causes stress, which causes early aging. Yoga and meditation can help you live a longer, happier life by combating this natural tendency. Once you've mastered those skills, you'll want to share their transformational abilities with others.

Libra

Everything should be in balance. That's you, and you're in luck when it comes to elegant aging. It is simple for you to live a happy and healthy lifestyle. You enjoy meeting new people and value having a significant relationship in your life. If that's what it takes, you'll be the first person on a dating site in your 60s. You also like intellectual and creative hobbies, which bodes well for maintaining mental acuity.

Scorpio

Scorpios never appear to age, whether it's due to strong genes or discipline. While everyone else's bodies begin to come apart around you, yours will strangely remain intact. Be modest about it, lucky woman, and continue to exercise, hydrate, and eat well on a regular basis. Avoid the seclusion that you may crave at times. You're in desperate need of people, and you have a lot to offer. Volunteering is an excellent option for you.

Sagittarius

Your active lifestyle may provide for a smooth transition into your older years, or it may make for a difficult one. You get to pick how your innate go-getter instinct manifests itself in a lifestyle that is either advantageous or harmful to your aging. Remember that setting and achieving objectives is what you excel at, and that once you make up your mind to accomplish anything, you'll follow through. Traveling is a great way to stay youthful.

Capricorn

Your work ethic and no-nonsense approach have served you well throughout your life, and they continue to serve you well now. You've taken good care of your body and mind, as well as your funds, and you're determined to see 101 through to the conclusion. However, it is beneficial to not take yourself so seriously all of the time. Being able to laugh and kick up your heels is an important part of aging gracefully.

Chapter 2

End of life symptoms

Caring for a loved one as they approach death is never easy. You're probably wondering what to anticipate, whether you're in charge of everything or just want to be there for them.

Learning about end-of-life symptoms in older persons can help you understand what your loved one is going through and make the transition easier for everyone.

Timeline of end-of-life symptoms
You shouldn't expect to observe all of these end-of-life indicators because everyone is different. Furthermore, your loved one will improve at their own rate, which may be extremely quick or extremely slow.

Several weeks before the end of life
A sense of resignation is one of the first indications to appear. Low mood, motivation, and withdrawal are all possible symptoms. The individual may devote more time to reminiscing about their upbringing and previous life experiences.

There is a loss of appetite, overall weakness, and growing weariness.

Days before one's death
It's possible that your loved one will sleep more than they'll be awake. They'll move and talk less, and they might not respond to noise or conversation. Their hearing is most likely unaffected, but their eyesight may be.

Other symptoms to look for in the latter days include:

Blood pressure, heart rate, and body temperature all decline.

Hallucinations, illusions, or delusions hallucinations, illusions, or delusions trouble swallowing rejecting food no more bowel motions or urine hallucinations, illusions, or delusions hallucinations, illusions, or delusions
Some people get a feeling of restlessness or a rush of energy.

Several hours before the end of life
The following are signs that the body is actively shutting down:

Breathing problems and a greater gap between breaths (Cheyne-Stokes breathing) breathing loudly
chilly extremities, glassy eyes
Knees, feet, and hands have purple, gray, pallid, or blotchy skin.
Changes in awareness, unexpected outbursts, and unresponsiveness are all symptoms of a weak pulse.

Hearing is regarded to be the last sense to deteriorate. Your loved one can most likely hear you even if you are unconscious.

At the moment of death
Breathing stops and there is no pulse or detectable blood pressure when someone dies. The pupils will dilate if the eyes remain open.

The bowels and bladder empty when the body's muscles relax. The skin becomes pallid and waxy as the blood settles.

Tears may continue fall from the eyes after death, as well as minor movements of the limbs, legs, or voice box.

Symptoms of impending death

1. Changes in appetite and digestion
As one gets closer to death, one's metabolism and digestion slow down.

Because fewer calories are required, appetite reduction and decreased thirst are common.

Swallowing difficulties, sickness, and constipation can all affect appetite. There might be indicators of dehydration and weight loss.

2. Getting more sleep

Weakness and tiredness on a broad scale are prevalent. As energy levels drop, so does the amount of time spent sleeping.

3. Isolation from the rest of the world

A sense of resignation and retreat from the greater world may be apparent. The individual may establish a protective bubble with fewer individuals and less interest in happenings outside the bubble. It's possible that they'll spend more time discussing the past than the present.

4. Anxiety and depression are two of the most common mental illnesses.
As the end of life approaches, some people become increasingly fearful or concerned for themselves or others who will be left behind. Anxiety and despair at the end of life are prevalent.

5. Bladder and urinary incontinence
Urine might become more concentrated and darker in color when the kidneys fail. Controlling bladder and bowel motions becomes more difficult.

6. Variations in vital signs
The heart rate, body temperature, and blood pressure all start to decline. The hands, arms, feet, and legs become chilly to the touch as circulation is diminished. The skin may become dark blue, purple, or mottled in appearance.

7. Perplexity

Your loved one may become perplexed from time to time. It might be difficult to pinpoint a certain time, location, or even close relatives. You may notice a short attention span or repeated gestures such as pulling blankets or tugging on clothes.

Changes in the senses
Eyesight is deteriorating. Someone on the verge of death may see, hear, or feel things you don't, and may even communicate with individuals who have passed on. Illusions, hallucinations, and delusions can all be caused by sensory alterations.

9. Bidding farewell

Some individuals wish to help with funeral arrangements, putting affairs in order, or dispersing belongings if they are aware of what is going on. They may feel compelled to tie up loose ends, express sentiments, and say their goodbyes.

10. Changes in breathing

With episodes of shortness of breath, breathing becomes progressively sluggish and shallow. As the throat muscles relax, fluid can accumulate in the throat. It's possible that the individual is too weak to cough it out, resulting in loud breathing known as "death rattle."

11. Consciousness loss

It might be tough to wake up a loved one. They'll eventually become unresponsive and uncommunicative, losing consciousness or succumbing to delirium. It's possible that your eyes will get watery.

How can you help your loved ones towards the end of their lives?
Based on their medical problems, your doctor will advise you on how to give physical comfort. This might involve giving painkillers, digestive aids, or anti-anxiety drugs.

Providing physical assistance

There are several fundamental techniques to provide physical comfort whether you have professional caregivers or hospice care:

To make breathing easier, use a humidifier.
Soothe dry skin with lip balm and alcohol-free lotion.
Ice chips or a moist towel on the lips might help them keep hydrated.
To avoid bedsores, change positions every few hours.

Comfortable bedding should be provided, and it should be refreshed as needed.
Prepare soft meals but do not compel someone to consume them.
Reduce the amount of light in the room and turn off any loud or distracting noises.
Allow them to sleep whenever they want.
Providing emotional relief

To assist in the provision of emotional and spiritual support:

If they're willing to talk, encourage it. Allow them to take the lead, be a good listener, and refrain from bringing up potentially difficult themes.
Assume they heard you, even if they don't answer. Instead of speaking about them, speak directly to them. When you enter or leave the room, identify yourself.

Hold their hand or place a hand on their shoulder to make gentle physical contact.
Reduce the volume of their favorite music.
Don't disregard, interrupt, or ignore what they're thinking. If they're perplexed, be cool. Allow them to converse with or see someone who isn't present.
Make your feelings known.
Don't pretend that something isn't true. Allow them to say their goodbyes if they so choose. It may provide you both peace of mind and security.

Consider your loved one's spiritual requirements. Bring in a spiritual counselor, social worker, or end-of-life doula if necessary.

Takeaway

It's not simple to let go. Understanding end-of-life symptoms in the elderly can assist you in providing the physical and emotional assistance your loved one requires as they transition.

Allow yourself time to grieve, take care of yourself, and get support if you need it after your loved one has died.

Chapter 3

What love means when you're old

"Yearning is never too old." —Italian adage
Older individuals, contrary to common assumption, are typically happier and more romantically engaged than younger ones. However, the nature of these romantic bonds may vary.
Happiness and maturity

"It's thrilling to experience mature tranquility. I'm enthralled by my elder partners' peace and acceptance, who live in the now rather than planning for the future." — A man in his thirties who enjoys dating women in their fifties.

Along with a decline in bodily and mental health, it was thought that

With aging, cerebral abilities, contentment, and romantic love all deteriorate.

We've learned our lesson. Older individuals are frequently happier and more content.

younger people are more content with their life and relationships

are.

Perhaps when we know how short our lives are, we will be more appreciative of what we have.

Change our viewpoint and concentrate on the good things that are happening right now.

ences, which are more likely to be serene and tranquil.

rather than excitement and delight, choose tranquility. Lyubomirsky, Sonja

(2013) summarizes these data, stating that many people believe that

The finest years of one's life are in the second half of one's life. Nevertheless,

There's a lot of variety here, as well as some older items.

People grow melancholy and fearful of death as a result of their experiences.

Maturity appears to be at odds with novelty and excitement. It's no surprise that young individuals are thought to be more emotional than older folks. This isn't to say that fascinating good and unpleasant events don't happen to people of all ages. Change elicits strong emotions, but maturation is becoming acclimated to changes and seeing them as less relevant.

Although we like both familiarity and novelty at all ages, the proportional importance of familiarity grows as we become older.

Mogilner et al. (2011) define pleasure linked with passionate love as exhilaration, whereas happiness connected with profound, mature love is described as peacefulness (calmness) and serenity.

The transition from adolescence to adulthood is marked by a change in strong

social relationships, as well as a shift in focus from quantity to quality. It has been claimed that resolving disagreements is the key develop mental work for younger couples, whereas sustaining mutual support is the main develop mental challenge for older couples (Carmichael et al., 2015).
Compromises and maturity
"You can't always get what you want, but if you try occasionally, you might just discover / You get what you need" —The Rolling Stones

We give up a romantic value, such as intense love, in return for a nonromantic quality-of-life value in romantic compromises. Compromise arises from the recognition that we are finite beings who cannot always satisfy our standards or realize our ambitions.

Survival often necessitates being adaptable, accepting something less—or just different—than we had hoped for.

circumstance. However, unlike maturity, compromise acceptance is mostly a behavioral rather than an attitude acceptance. As long as the situation is still considered a compromise, the individual does not truly embrace it. When individuals embrace a compromise entirely, it ceases to be a compromise.
Love that has matured

"At an advanced age, romantic vistas do actually narrow; there are undoubtedly fewer numerical and emotional options." This leads to many people staying in their comfort zones and refusing to engage in a relationship, or expecting a relationship to happen to them without them having to do anything." —Marano, Hara Estroff
mature, since settling for the possible while rejecting the desired might indicate a loss of excitement and spontaneity. When individuals compromise, however, they do just that.

We want youngsters to grow up and learn to appreciate long-term considerations, while we want elderly folks to be less concerned about long-term risks and to express their feelings more freely.

We don't want to lose our happy, childlike qualities. We want to be upbeat and real, and we want to love deeply. Despite our evident imperfections, we want to appreciate each other.

We want to understand each other well, but we also want to see each other in a positive light so that we can work together.

We can be deceived by optimistic illusions. We want to keep the buoyancy, naturalness, and ardor that we associate with children while still being mature adults who support each other through the inevitable suffering that comes with long-term love relationships. We seek to solve issues by altering our perceptions and attitudes toward one another, rather than by changing each other.

People that act immaturely are really appealing: they are incredibly vivacious, cheerful, and youthful, living in the moment as if it were their last. They are, however, frequently unpredictable and unstable, making you question if they will love you tomorrow when they meet someone else. Having an interesting son allows them to completely experience romantic life from a different perspective.

Love at a later age

"Love is the term used to describe the young's sexual enthusiasm, the middle-habituation, aged's and the elderly's mutual dependence." —Ciardi, John

"Extramarital relationships are an expression of a stubborn reluctance to age gracefully." Catherine Hakim is a writer who lives in New York City.

Old people, according to popular belief, are incapable of feeling great love since their sexual drive and physical powers are assumed to have waned with age. This is a twisted and oversimplified concept. Love at an older age is frequently deeper than love at a younger age.

It is a weaker predictor of cognitive abilities and conduct in later life (although incomplete). The subjective feeling of our remaining time before death is an additional temporal feature that becomes more essential than the period since our birth.

The length of our horizons in terms of time has a significant impact on motivation. Carstensen claims that as individuals get older, they begin to perceive time as limiting and their horizons as narrowing. As a result, their priorities shift. For example, they place less emphasis on objectives that broaden their horizons and place a higher emphasis on goals that provide immediate emotional value.

Older adults have fewer social connections, are less interested in novelty, and have smaller domains of interest than younger ones. They appear to be as happy as (if not happier than) younger folks. This makes sense, because individuals prioritize expanding existing connections and growing skill in already enjoyable areas of life when their horizons are shrinking (Carstensen, 2006).

Elderly couples appear to be more willing to adopt a happy-go-lucky attitude. Consider this confession from a sinful mother in her fifties: "I'm searching for perfection, and I've made mistakes in my decisions."

I refuse to spend time with males because I believe they are far from flawless. I'm softening as I get older, but I'm also becoming more clear about what I enjoy and want. I don't want to seem shallow, but for the first time in my life, I'm thinking about having sex with someone who isn't partner material!" married couples may have less marital issues than their younger counterparts, but sexual relationships are less important in their lives. The cardinal element of their interactions appears to be

companionate love, which is founded on friendship. Intimate relationships are reasonably peaceful and rewarding in old age (Charles & Carstensen, 2002).
As we become older, romantic concessions become less of a problem. People become used to their spouse's bad characteristics over time. They learn to live with them while reducing their negative consequences.
When we understand that time is running out and our options are dwindling, we are more inclined to accept our limitations and not feel betrayed by not pursuing a more appealing choice.

Furthermore, when people become older and become more reliant on one another, marriage shackles tend to transform into helping hands. Older adults may be more robust in the face of conflicts in their closest relationships, while feeling as much negativity as younger people. Older folks are better at putting the issue into context (Charles & Carstensen, 2010).

Finally, some thoughts

"It's the first time in my life that I'm becoming old." I've never known what it's like to grow old." —Naomi Polani Polani Polani Polani Polani Polani Pol

It appears that when one's cognitive and physical skills deteriorate with age, one's capacity to be content with one's own lot improves, reducing marital disputes and the feeling of romantic compromise. Older folks are more prone to take the proactive approach of making the most of what they have.